JACK KEROUAC
POMES ALL SIZES

INTRODUCTION BY ALLEN GINSBERG

THE POCKET POETS SERIES #48

CITY LIGHTS BOOKS

SAN FRANCISCO

POMES ALL SIZES © 1992 by John Sampas, Literary Representative
Introduction © 1992 by Allen Ginsberg

Cover: *Kerouac*. Painting by Lawrence Ferlinghetti, 1990.
       Courtesy of Dennis Q. Sullivan
Cover Design: John Miller, Big Fish Books
Typesetting: Jeff Brandenburg, ImageComp
Production Coordination: Eric Houts

Library of Congress Cataloging-in-Publication Data

Kerouac, Jack, 1922-1969.
        [Poems. Selections]
        Pomes all sizes / by Jack Kerouac.
                p.   cm. — (Pocket poets series ; no. 48)
        ISBN 0-87286-269-0 : $10.95
        I. Title.
Ps3521.E735A6 1992
811'.54—dc20

                                                        92-1204
                                                        CIP

City Lights Books are available to bookstores through our primary
distributor: Subterranean Company, P.O. Box 160, 265 S. 5th St.,
Monroe, OR 97456. 541-847-5274 Toll-free orders 800-274-7826. FAX
541-847-6018. Our books are also available through library jobbers and
regional distributors. For personal orders and catalogs, please write to
City Lights Books, 261 Columbus Avenue, San Francisco, CA 94133.

CITY LIGHTS BOOKS are edited by Lawrence Ferlinghetti and
Nancy J. Peters and published at the City Lights Bookstore,
261 Columbus Avenue, San Francisco, CA 94133.

CONTENTS

INTRODUCTION

BY ALLEN GINSBERG

Part I

KEROUAC'S *POMES ALL SIZES*

He was Poet: — *You guys call yourselves poets, write little short lines, I'm a poet but I write lines paragraphs and pages and many pages long.* Thus he wrote in mid-50s, a letter from Mexico City enclosing a scroll of his *Blues.*

Thus his ear auditing Burroughs' naked prose poetry: "Motel motel motel loneliness moans along still oily tidal waters of East Texas bayous . . . "

His ear followed the road of sound: " . . . the mad road, keening in a seizure of tarpaulin power." He didn't know what the phrase meant, as he wrote it, later realized that "tarpaulin" covered truck gondolas piled with logs or pipes.

His ear came from reading and music: Thomas Wolfe, Herman Melville, Shakespeare, C.F. Atkinson's translation of Spengler's Germanic portentous sound in *The Decline of the West,* Sir Thomas Browne, Rabelais, Shelley, Poe, Hart Crane — a romantic ear. And modern Whitman, Eliot, Pound, Céline and Genet. Soul from Dostoyevsky and Gogol. Music from Bach's "St. Matthew Passion" to Thelonious Monk's "Mysterioso."

His influence is worldwide, not only in spirit, with beat planetary Youth Culture, but poetic, technical. It woke Bob Dylan to world minstrelry: "How do you know Kerouac's poetry?" I asked Mr. Dylan after we improvised songs and read some *Mexico City Blues* choruses over Kerouac's gravestone 1976 Lowell's Edison Cemetery, cameras on us walking side by side under high trees and shifting clouds as we disappeared down distant aisles of gravestones. Dylan's answer: *Someone handed me* Mexico City Blues *in St. Paul in 1959 and it blew my mind.* He said it was the first poetry that spoke his own language.

My own poetry's always been modeled on Kerouac's practice of tracing his mind's thoughts and sounds directly on the page. Poetry can be "writing the mind," the Ven. Chögyam Trungpa phrased it, corollary to his slogan "First thought, best thought," itself parallel to Kerouac's formulation "Mind is shapely, Art is shapely." Reading *Mexico City Blues* to that great Buddhist teacher from the front carseat on a long drive Karme Chöling Retreat Center (1972 called Tail of the Tiger) to New York, Trungpa laughed all the way as he listened: "Anger doesn't like to be reminded of fits . . . . The wheel of the quivering meat conception . . . . The doll-like way she stands / bow-legged in my dreams waiting to serve me . . . . Don't ignore other parts of the mind . . . . " As we got out of the car he stood on the pavement and said, *It's a perfect exposition of mind.*

The next day he told me, *I kept hearing Kerouac's voice all night, or yours and Anne Waldman's . . . .* It'd given him a new idea of American poetry, for his own poetry — thus Trungpa Rinpoche's last decade's open-form international spontaneous style *First Thought Best Thought* poetry collection. Thus two years later the "Jack Kerouac School of Disembodied Poetics" was founded with Naropa Institute, certainly a center for meeting of classical Eastern wisdom meditative practice with Western alert spontaneous candid thought, healthy synthesis of Eastern and Western Mind, at last these twain've met forever Hallelujah Svaha!

But back to America in mid-50s — the scroll of *Mexico City Blues* mailed to our cottage in Berkeley inspired poet Philip Whalen to write "Big Baby Buddha Golden 65 feet high" ("Big high song for somebody"). Philip Lamantia, authentic surrealist American poet, had already delighted in Kerouac's catholic tender mind Big Sur 1950 on Peyote.

Gary Snyder preparing to go to Japan was impressed by Kerouac's intuitive familiarity with Dharma sutra and its manifestation in *Blues*: *When I first saw* Mexico City Blues *I was immediately taken by the ease of it, the effortless way it moved on — apparently effortless — at the same time there was some constant surprise arising in the words, always something happening with the words. You can see the mind at work, see the mind in it. Each poem was complete in itself, each had a similar mode of movement, each like a little stanza born. In the year [1955] I was getting to know Jack, I was touched by* Mexico City Blues *and Whitman, the same influence at that time, struck by poems Kerouac published in the Berkeley* Bussei.

Michael McClure was inspired to the later ditties of *September Blackberries*. *It's the sheer beauty of his treatment of everyday divine world . . . . the smallest voice was equal to the most heroic chunk of matter. . . . In addition I was illuminated, thrilled, deeply moved by seeing the natural unplanned growth of them, poem after poem, each with a life of its own . . . . There's a movement thru space of an energy, a system that acts to organize that system. You see Kerouac's flow, you can follow his spiritual energy as the system moves along acting to organize itself into a great religious poem. He's* the model from which the spirit drives outward organizing itself into a *previously nonexistent structure* — *equivalent to life, it's like a living being,* Mexico City Blues.

All San Francisco Renaissance poets were curious, interested, impressed, sometimes inspired by Kerouac's solitary autocthonous strength, ear, Kerouac's sound, his unobstructed grasp of American idiom. Thus Robert Duncan's astonishment at Kerouac's "Belief and Technique for Modern Prose: List of Essentials" I'd tacked on my wall when he visited Marconi Hotel, North Beach 1955.

Robert Creeley speaks of that time: *Jack had an extraordinary ear, that impeccable ear that could hear patterns and make patterns in the sounds and rhythms of the language as spoken. Extraordinary ear, in the way he could manage such a live and insistently natural structure. Jack was a genius at the register of the speaking voice, a human voice talking. Its effect on my poetry? He gave an absolute measure of what the range of that kind of writing was.*

Before that, the standards ranged from Cummings to Prévert, but with Kerouac we had a human voice, not as imitation, but as fact of that voice talking. That he could do it in both poetry and prose interested me.

Same confusion of critics as with Lawrence, the constant problem of falling between two stools, prose and poetry. He was classified as novelist despite the evidence of "October in the Railroad Earth," Mexico City Blues, *and* Visions of Cody *that the distinction between the two forms was in certain writers artificial — they are inseparable. Kerouac's simultaneous ability in prose and poetry, like Hardy, like Lawrence, like Joyce, like Jean Genet, like Burroughs, proposes questions that are more fruitful to contemplate than to dismiss . . . .*

Kerouac was a writer, as Burroughs remarked; that is, he *wrote*. He practiced writing, and for him writing was a sacred practice as he himself prayed, "I made a supplication in this dream." Holy recollected visions of mortal existence with panoramic scope of suffering and transitoriness — Buddhist sympathy and Catholic compassion — gave motif constantly lofty and playful — the very mind of poetry. So Olson championed Kerouac from a distance. And Lew Welch drove across American with him, writing Haiku.

The second generation of New York school, well-versed in the spontaneous sophistications of O'Hara and Ashbery, recognized Kerouac's genius and were influenced by this American spontaneity — Ted Berrigan and Aram Saroyan notably, who interviewed him for *Paris Review*; Tom Clark and Anne Waldman, themselves powers at St. Mark's Poetry Project, inherited some of Kerouac's energy and intelligence in U.S. ordinary mind — sacred mind, pop art mind, Bop mind. And Leroi Jones (Amiri Baraka), who liberated a world of African-American verse, also caught some of Jack Kerouac's mind and musical vibration and publicly praised Kerouac's theoretic rationale of authentic oral spontaneity. And certainly it was Kerouac who collaborated with William Burroughs in Burroughs' first "hardboiled" fiction back in 1945 and passed the romantic "gemlike flame" of sacred prose-poetry, home-made, personal, spontaneous, to Burroughs himself: Kerouac was a catalyst there. And how many would-be poets, ordinary poets, and genius poets in U.S. found Kerouac's legend and texts a model inspiration?

Certainly a colossus, for his poetry books and parallel prose poetry passages in novels (whether in still-life sketches of first 150 pages of *Visions of Cody,* or the Shroud at the window of *Dr Sax,* or the ear babble of "Old Angel Midnight") or the haiku, playful snapshots & matured musings in the present posthumously published *Pomes All Sizes.* Kerouac is a major, perhaps seminal, poet of the latter half of U.S. XX Century — and mayhap thru his imprint on Dylan and myself among others, a poetic influence over the entire planet. Jack Kerouac was above all a poet's poet, as well as a people's poet and an Ivory Tower poet, like Rimbaud legended to youth round the world.

Alas a poet not yet appreciated by the Academy as represented by major college Anthologies used in the quarter century or so since Kerouac's death 1969. Nineteen-sixties' *New American Poetry* introduced Kerouac to the world of Anthology (as well as myself, O'Hara, Ashbery, Corso, Koch, Olson, Creeley, Lamantia, Wieners, Snyder, Levertov, et al.). Following that — total amnesia! But look in 1990s' Norton, Macmillan, Harvard, Oxford, Heath, etc. etc. textbooks lined up row after row in College Bookstores, arriving at English Department mailboxes, heavy tomes authored by Professors from sea to shining sea, published with groaning labor, we find poet after poet influenced consciously by Kerouac, or swept up unconsciously into the cultural stream of self-empowerment — initiated by Kerouac — academic poets with loosened verse, minority poets of all colors indebted to Kerouac's bardic breakthru — But where's a text of Kerouac? Nowhere to be found to astonish and delight youngsters who open these classroom books. Mediocre poets mix with modern great names, experimental poets mix with re-formalist pigmies, first-rate ordinary versifiers mix with multicultural identity boosters. But Kerouac the author-catalyst of this American Literary Revolution? Not yet to be found in "establishment" Anthologies!

He'll be read in volumes like this, which Kerouac himself prepared before his death for City Lights Books, publisher of his outlandish classic original *Book of Dreams* (1961), and first posthumous *Scattered Poems* (1971). Lawrence Ferlinghetti speaks: *I was influenced by Kerouac, not in the 50s by* Mexico City Blues, *but years later. I stole quite a few images from him — I've used that "quivering meat wheel". . . . I remember, from Jack's French poems, I picked up on how you can blend the French and English, and I did that in some of my poems. He's a hero to French Canadian writers, not only to prose writers but also brother to Québecois poets.*

Here's a treasure — in the mainstream of American Literature, random as this collection is, of notebook jottings, little magazine items — containing lovely familiar classic Kerouacisms, nostalgic gathas from 1955 Berkeley cottage days, pure sober tender Kerouac of your yore, pithy exquisite later drunken laments and bitter nuts and verses. *Pomes All Sizes* — modest title — to be appreciated by cognoscenti and literate strangers — more valuable for being *isolato*, original, unrecognized, exactly because such beauty's too personal to be noticed by literature's officialdom — "mis-noticed" — sociopolitically "inconvenient" to include in the exasperating parade of college-wise-notable acceptable poetry collections by professionals and editors.

"This prophecy Merlin shall make for I live before his time:" 'Till Kerouac as poet's understood, his formal verse beauty visible to scholars, and his surprise mind tenderness taken straight-forwardly and felt by vulnerable Professors, the teaching of American literature'll never get on the right track, a conscious breath of U.S. poetry be neglected, the nation won't exhale its own compassionate spirit, hordes of literary bureaucrats will continue to snuffle shallow inspiration and new generations'll be turned off to Poetry except for individual chance in finding this original Kerouac book or works by Kerouac fellow traveler poets like-minded and lighthearted on the same road announced by Walt Whitman.

New Year's Day 1992

Part II

Retrospect on Beat Generation

Meditating, still thinking of Kerouac's role as Dharma Bodhisattva Bringer or Messenger in *Mexico City Blues*, and after conversation with Wm. Burroughs at 4:00 pm, inquiring Jack's catalytic effect in encouraging Bill to write — also having inspected Ann Charters' Viking Portable Library 1992 *Beat Reader*, ruminated: —

That the quality most pure in Kerouac was his grasp that life is really a dream ("a dream already ended," he wrote) as well as being real, both real and dream, both at the same time — a deep insight that cut through knots of artificial intellect, extremism, totalitarian rationality, "new reasons for spitefulness," cut through all the basic vanity, resentment, & wrongheadedness that cursed most XX-Century political and literary movements — or weakened them with impermanent grounding or stained them with the fog of misdirection. That realization of dream as the suchness of this universe pervaded the spiritual intelligence of all Beat writers on differing levels, whether Burroughs' suspicion of all "apparent sensory phenomena"; Herbert

Huncke's *Evening Sun Turned Crimson*; Corso's paradoxical wit (viz., "Death hiding beneath the kitchen sink: 'I'm not real' it cried, 'I'm just a rumor spread by Life,' " a late paradox, or his earlier "Dirty Ears aims a knife at me / I pump him full of lost watches"); or Orlovsky's compassionate view of Minnerbia, "Her teeth-brush dream is the one she loves best"; or Snyder's meditations in mind wilderness; or Sensei Whalen's pithy aphorisms, "Poetry is a graph of the mind moving"; or McClure's insight into the gnat, "Nature abhors a vacuum"; or Lamantia's *Ecstasis* prophecy, "I long for the / it is nameless that I long for"; even John Wieners' heavy woe's the work of conscious dreamer, "Particles of light / worshipped in the pitches of the night."

But the doctrine of consciousness of Sunyatā, emptiness, with all its transcendental wisdom including panoramic awareness, oceanic city vastness, a humoresque appreciation of minute details of the big dream, especially "character in the bleak inhuman aloneness" in "Memorial Cello Time" is most clearly and consistently set forth in the body of Kerouac's prose, poetry, and essays.

This basic metaphysical understanding of the eternal nature of dream, more or less clearly perceived by the various "Beat" authors according to their individual temperaments, served as common ground and saved their essential work from the decay of time — because the "message" was permanent, as "change" and "emptiness" are a permanent gnosis from Heraclitus' time to now. As Beauty itself is the realization of simultaneous "emptiness" & "form," the co-emergent wisdom of Buddhadharma.

"Come back and tell me in a hundred years," Kerouac commanded — his koan.

"What was the face you had before you were born?" — that question was always at the heart of Beat poetry. It could be called the "Golden Ash" school, as Kerouac qualified existence. Thus Beat: "a dream already ended . . . " Thus beatific, "the Golden Ash" of dream. One could call this Heart Failure a big success.

1/8/92

BUS EAST

Poem written on a bus April 1954
from S.F. to New York

BUS EAST

Society has good intentions
Bureaucracy is like a friend

5 years ago—other furies
   other losses—

America's trying
to control the
   uncontrollable
Forest fires,
   Vice

The essential smile
In the essential sleep
Of the children
Of the essential mind

 I'm all thru playing
   the American
 Now I'm going to
   live a good quiet life

1

The world should be
built for foot walkers

Oily rivers
Of spiney   Nevady

I am Jake Cake
            Rake
Write like Blake

   The horse is not
       pleased
    Sight of his
gorgeous finery
    in the dust
Its silken nostrils
    did disgust

Cats arent kind
Kiddies arent sweet

April in Nevada—
Investigatin Dismal Cheyenne
Where the war parties
In fields of straw
Aimed over oxen
  At Indian Chiefs
In wild headdress

2

Pouring thru the gap
In Wyoming plain
To make the settlers
Eat more dust
  than dust was eaten
In the States
  From East at Seacoast
Where wagons made up
  To dreadful Plains
Of clazer vup

Saltry settlers
Anxious to masturbate
  The Mongol Sea
    (I'm too tired
      in Cheyenne—No
    sleep in 4 nights now, &
      2 to go)

NEBRASKA

April doesnt hurt here
Like it does in New England
The ground
Vast and brown
Surrounds dry towns
Located in the dust
Of the coming locust

3

Live for survival, not for "kicks"

Be a bangtail describer,
like of shrouded traveler
in Textile tenement &
  the birds fighting in yr
  ears—like Burroughs
  exact to describe &
  gettin $

The Angry Hunger
(hunger is anger
  who fears
  the hungry
  feareth
  the angry)

And so I came home
To Golden far away
Twas on the horizon
Every blessed day
As we rolled
And we rolled
From Donner tragic Pass
Thru April in Nevada
And out Salt City Way
Into the dry Nebraskas
And sad Wyomings

4

Where young girls
And pretty lover boys
With Mickey Mantle eyes
Wander under moons
Sawing in lost cradle
And Judge O Fastera
Passes whiggling by
To ask of young love:
"Was it the same wind
Of April Plains eve
that ruffled the dress
  Of my lost love
  Louanna
  In the Western
  Far off night
    Lost as the whistle
    Of the passing Train
    Everywhere West
    Roams moaning
  The deep basso
—Vom! Vom!
—Was it the same love
Notified my bones
As mortify yrs now
Children of the soft
Wyoming April night?
  Couldna been!
  But was! But was!"

And on the prairie
The wildflower blows
In the night
For bees & birds
And sleeping hidden
Animals of life.

Then Chicago
Spitters in the spotty street
Cheap beans, loop,
Girls made eyes at me
And I had 35
Cents in my jeans—

Then Toledo
Springtime starry
Lover night
Of hot rod boys
And cool girls
A wandering
A wandering
In search of April pain
A plash of rain
Will not dispel
This fumigatin hell
Of lover lane
This park of roses
Blue as bees

In former airy poses
In aerial O Way hoses
No tamarand
And figancine
Can the musterand
Be less kind
  Sol—
  Sol—
 Bring forth yr
 Ah Sunflower—
 Ah me Montana
 Phosphorescent Rose
 And bridge in
  fairly land
I'd understand it all—

HITCHHIKER

"Tryna get to sunny Californy"—
　　　　Boom. It's the awful raincoat
making me look like a selfdefeated self-
murdering imaginary gangster, an idiot in
a rueful coat, how can they understand
my damp packs—my mud packs—
　　　　"Look John, a hitchhiker"
　　　　"He looks like he's got a gun underneath
that I.R.A. coat"
　　　　"Look Fred, that man by the road"
　　　　"Some sexfiend got in print in 1938
in Sex Magazine"—
　　　　"You found his blue corpse in a
greenshade edition, with axe blots"

NEAL IN COURT

All Neal's life has been hard
And harsh
People dont believe him
And he's all alone
Look at his bones
In courthouse scenes
And look at the pictures
Of his railroad track
And judge
And have secret witnesses
Against his misery

Raven, Craven,
Nobody cares—
Hate to lose their jobs
Put old Cassady in jail

But he sits bong Buddha
Hands Catholic crossed
In the witness chair

And the afternoon wears on
In the schoolhouse kiddy court
Of old black velvet angels

With white hair
And tassels in their caps

He did make the joint;
Facts of Coupling;
"You give a sign
 To the engineer"

He's got them beat
With his young composure

Exhibit No. 4
Shows the long ladder
And the brake
Platform
Where he fell & cracked his ankle

He nods & listens patiently
To the prosecutor's counsel
Smiling speaking civilly
For the society of ladies
And respect of settlements
And has an aging chin.
The Jewish stenographess
 Writes unconcerned

In silent machine shorthand
And watches sexily

The lips of speaking men
And frowns to catch the last word
Spoken in Eternity
Eyes gazed on suit lapel
And burping to look down—

Papers rustle, people cough
   Ivan's not here to turn
        all pale
Nor Dmitri but to shout
"You all tried to kill
        yr fathers
The Immemorial Lout!"
So have another beer
        Neal
Your money
        big or small'll
Come
And when come
   You only have a few more
        years
Like Raven
        more or less
   To hang on—

For you've done it all before
In Millbrae & in Burlingame
In Samarkand, Chandrapore,

Jamie, Cathy, Johnny
All were there—
Redwood, Belmont, & Nameless
        too—
  Harsh harbors, duties,—
  Flower cars—& bums—
  Dont let the punk
  In smart brown suit
  Who cant lick you
  In street fight
  Screw you out of thousands
  In this million years
  Of strife, the Moose
  of heaven's looking down.

East end of the rail
West end of the Ram
The stars are looking down
On all yr pain & tears
  And Allen Ginsberg loves you
  And Carolyn too
  Let old Raven lie
  We'll hang him in the sea

Fog will kiss him
Make him shiver
Bones'll belie
His coral deficiency

Insincere & sad
The world's a farce
To stand and sneer at
On the corner of
      Snark & Phnark

March 30, 1954,
San Francisco City Hall

BOWERY BLUES

by Jean-Louis

> For I
> Prophesy
> That the night
> Will be bright
> With the gold
> Of old
> In the inn
> Within.

Cooper Union Cafeteria—late cold March afternoon, the street (Third Avenue) is cobbled, cold, desolate with trolley tracks— Some man on the corner is waving his hand down No-ing somebody emphatically and out of sight behind a black and white pillar, cold clowns in the moment horror of the world—A Porto Rican kid with a green stick, stooping to bat the sidewalk but changing his mind and halting on—Two new small trucks parked—The withery gray rose stone building across the street with its rime heights in the quiet winter sky, inside are quiet workers by neon entablatures practicing fanning lessons with the murderous Marbo—A yakking blonde with awful wide smile is making her mouth lip talk to an old Bodhisattva papa on the sidewalk, the tense quickness of her hard working words—Meanwhile a funny bum with no sense tries to panhandle them and is waved away

14

stumbling, he doesnt care about society women embarrassed with paper bags on sidewalks—Unutterably sad the broken winter shattered face of a man passing in the bleak ripple—Followed by a Russian boxer with an expression of Baltic lostness, something grim and Slavic and so helplessly beyond my conditional ken or ability to evaluate and believe that I shudder as at the touch of cold stone to think of him, the sickened old awfulness of it like slats of wood wall in an old brewery truck

> Shin McOntario with
> no money, no bets, no
> health, palls on by
> pawing his inside coat
> no hope of ever
> seeing Miama again
> since he lost his pickles
> on Orchard Street
> and his father
> S t u h t e l f e d e h r e d
> him to hospitals
> Of gray
> bleak
> bone
> drying
> in the moon
> that mortifies his coat
> and words sing

what mind
brings
Bleeding bloody seamen
Of Indian England
Battering in coats
Of Third Ave noo
With no sense and their brows
Streaked with wine sop
Blood of ogligit
Sad adventurers
Far from the pipe
Of Liverpool
The bean of bone
Bottle Liffey brown
Far   hung   unseen
Top tippers
Of ocean wave.
   God bless & sing for them
   As I can not

*

Cooper Union Blues,
The Musak is too Sod.
The gayety of grave
Candidates makes

My gut weep
And my brains
Are awash
Down the side of the
        blue orange table
As little sneery snirfling
Porto Rican hero
Bats by booming
His coat pocket
Fisting to the Vicinity
Where Mortuary
Waits for bait.
(What kind of service
Do broken barrels give?)
    O have pity
        Bodhisattva
        Of Intellectual
        Radiance!

Save the world from her eyebrows
Of beautiful illusion
Hope, O hope,
O Nope, O pope

                    *

Crowded coaters
In a front seat
Car, gray & grim,
Push on thru
To the basketball

*

Various absurd parades—
The strict in tact
Intent man with
Broken back
Balling his suitcase
Down from Washington
Building in the night
Passing little scaggly
Children with Ma's
Of mopey hope.

Too sad, too sad
The well kept
Clean cut
Ferret man.

And the old blue Irishman
With untenable dignity
Beer bellying home
To drowsy dowdy TV
Suppers of gravy
And bile—

18

Wearing old new coats
Meant to be smooth on youths
Wrinkled on his barrel
Like sea wind
Infatuating sea eyes
To thinkin
Ripples & old age
Are real.

*

Poor young husbandry
  With coat of tan
Digging change in palms
  For bleaker coffees
Than afternoon gloom
  Where work of stone
Was endowed
  With tired hope.
Hope   O hope
Cooper Union Hope
O Bowery of Hopes!
O absence!
O blittering real
Non staring redfaced
Wild reality!
Hiding in the night
Like my dead father

I see the crystal
Shavings shifting
Out of sight
Dropping pigeons of light
To the Turd World

Enough, sad ones—
False petals
Of pure lotus
In drugstore windows
Where cups of O
Are smoked

Paddy McGilligan
Muttering in the street
Just hit town
From Calci bleak

Ole Mop Polock Pat
Angry as a cat
About to stumble
Into the movie
Of the night
Through which he sees
Mooda lands
Un seen
Like waking in the night
To transcendental Milk
In the room

20

Sad Jewish respectable
rag men with trucks
And watchers
Shaking cloth
Into the gutter
Saying   I dunno,no,no,
As gray green hat
Sits on their heads
Protecting them
From Infinity above
Which shines with white
Wide & brown black clouds
As Liberty Sun
Honks over the Sea
Sending Ships
From inner sea
Free
To de rool york
Pock Town of Part
Shelf High Hawk
Man Dung Town.
   Rinkidink Charley is Crazy.

*

Ugly pig
Burping
In the sidewalk
As surrealistic
  Typewriters
  Swim singing by
  And bigger marines
  Lizard thru the side
  Of the gloom
  Like water
  For this
  is the Sea
  Of
  Reality.

                    *

The story of man
Makes me sick
Inside, outside,
I dont know why
Something so conditional
And all talk
Should hurt me so.

I am hurt
I am scared

I want to live
I want to die
I dont know
Where to turn
In the Void
And when
To cut
Out

For no Church told me
No Guru holds me
No advice
Just stone
Of New York
And on the cafeteria
We hear
The saxophone
O dead Ruby
Died of Shot
In Thirty Two,
Sounding like old times
And de bombed
Empty decapitated
Murder by the clock.
And I see Shadows
Dancing into Doom
In love, holding
Tight the lovely asses
Of the little girls

In love with sex
Showing themselves
In white undergarments
At elevated windows
Hoping for the Worst.

I cant take it
Anymore
If I cant hold
My little behind
To me in my room

Then it's goodbye
Sangsara
For me
Besides
Girls arent as good
As they look
And Samadhi
Is better
Than you think
When it starts in
Hitting your head
In with Buzz
Of glittergold
Heaven's Angels
Wailing
Saying

We ve been waiting for you
  Since Morning, Jack
—Why were you so long
   Dallying in the sooty room?
   This Transcendental Brilliance
   Is the better part
   (Of Nothingness
   I sing)

Okay.
Quit.
Mad.
Stop.

Mar 29, 1955, NY

Long Poem In Canuckian Child Patoi Probably Medieval

Robert, Robert, ta belle grosse mere
enterez dan l'beurre—
La j me rapele
La j me rapele

Robert, t'eta tit
Mais tu waite encore plus gros
Que tu l'est deja—
C'est toute un reve qu'arretera
Avant quon l'finisse—
Quand on laisse la Divinite
    le finir
    Robert, Robert—
Ou est ton arbre?
Quosse qu'on y faite avec tes
    Indes especialles?
A tu tombez dans un trou
    de tristesse avec moi
Dans la nuit commune
    et sale et pire que mal?
Robert, ou est ton beau
    frere? Tes tite ridresse,

26

ON WAKING FROM A DREAM
OF ROBERT FOURNIER

And this is an English Blues

Robert, Robert, yr beautiful big mother
buried in butter —
Now I remember
Now I remember

Robert, you were small
But you'll be yet bigger
Than you are already —
It's all a dream that'll end
Before we finish it —
When we let Divinity
    end it
    Robert, Robert —
Where is your grass?
What'd they do with your
    special nothingness?
Did you fall in a hole
    of sadness with me
In the common night
    and dirty and worse than bad?
Robert, where is yr beautiful
    brother? Yr little laughs,

27

laughage, riendresse, malheur'se
aise—ou est ton son?
Ou sont les neiges?
les etoiles eloignez?
Les Reves?

Ya des faces dans l'arbre
    qu'il nous moque pas.
Robert, tes fleurs, tes femmes,
    tes folles,—
    tes friandises de bines
    en cuisines.
    Es tu mort ton gros pere
    enterrez dans ma mer?
    "Dread drizzle mere, Robert.
        dread drizzle mere"
Je vue les armes de face
    vegetables, comme des
    picottes dans ma
    noirceur d yeux—
J'attend les ti fou
chantez leur musique
idiotique et tendre
et charmant comme
comediens de Vienne,
Chante dans sa cabane,
attend—

"laughage," nothingness, unhappy
ease—where is your sound?
Where are the snows?
the wandered stars?
The Dreams?

There are faces in the tree
   that do not mock us.
Robert, your flowers, your women,
   your madwomen,—
   your delicacies of beans
   in kitchens.
   Is he dead your big father
   buried in my sea?
   "Dread drizzle mere, Robert,
      dread drizzle mere"
I see the armies of faces
   vegetable, like
   pockmarks in my
   darkness of eyes—
I hear the little nuts
singing their music
idiotic and tender
and charming like
comedians of Vienne,
sings in his shack,
waits—

les rats mange sa granche
tandis qu'il chante!
Robert, Robert, les rats
mange son coeur, son
nom y'est Alain—
Alain nee Fournier
La chanson de Dieu ma
rentrez la oreilles assoir,
mon coeur, Robert, je veux
t'expliquer—
Fa pu de face souffrante
dans les bars brunes
Laisse plus les chiens t'mordre,
Offre leux plus ta patte
de pauvre brume, viens
avec moi au ciel pur,
ecoute
Je voue de coupures
de chair dan mon aise—
Mais c'est toute pardu
dans la meme luisante
ocean de l'amour de Dieu
L'amor de Dios—
Love of God—
J'ai ta mere par les mains,
Marie Louise, je la sord,
J'l a ma dan mon
l'eglise, j'y allume des

The rats eat his barn
while he sings!
Robert, Robert, the rats
    eat his heart, his
    name is Allen—
    Allen born Fournier
The song of God
came in my ears tonight,
my heart, Robert, I want
to explain to you—
    Make no more suffering grimaces
    in the brown bars
Don't let the dogs bite you any more,
Offer them no more your leg
Of poor mist, come
with me to the pure heaven,
    listen
    I see scars
    of flesh in my ease—
But it's all lost
in the same shining
ocean of the Love of God
L'amor de Dios—
    Love of God—
I have your mother by the hands,
Marie Louise, I bring her out,
I put her in my
church, I light her

fleur, j'la fa travaillez
pour le Bon Seigneur—
    est pas peur Robert,
    ame tendre et tranquil—
Ah c'est un reve pour
    cossez les chose bati,
    quoi d'autre?
    Vien avec moi
    Robert, assoir,
braille plus,—
    Rente avec moi dans
    les Indes—
Fini l'reve,—
Instruit ta mere, ton pere,
ton pauvre grand frere,
tes vieux freres du matin—
    Sort!—
    Monte!
    Ascend!
    Vas entour!
        Ou tu peu!
Sur la terre comme tu peu tu pu,
    pi c'est fini,—
Reve—inveiglez,
    emorfouillez, fou,
    candrassez,
    impossiblement vife
    et toignant—

flowers, I make her work
for the Good Lord—
 have no fear Robert,
 soul tender and tranquil—
Ah it's a dream to
 break things built,
 what else?
 Come with me
 Robert, tonight,
cry no more,—
 Come in with me
 into the Nothingnessess—
Finish the dream,—
Instruct your mother, your father,
your poor tall brother,
your old brothers of morning—
 Go out!
 Go up!
 Ascend!
 Go below!
  Where you can!
On earth as you may you stink,
 then it's finished—
Dream—inveigled,
 mortified, crazy,
 broken-up,
 impossibly quick
 and tugging—

Marde pour les chailles
    moronique du diable—
La Vie n'est Pas

Robert, Robert,
    je tu perdu
    dans la mer omnisce
    pour toujours
        dejas
            helas— !
Les vignes montres les potos,
Les hommes souffres—
    Les Bouddhes
        chante tranquilement
        entre tous—
La tristesse et la mort
    et l'amour false
    de jambes et larmes—
Sort!— Rentre!
Monte!   Cour!
    Dor!
Ecoute, Robert la priere
    du Seigneur—pour tue—
"O Robert—qui a la
    clef du pouvoire
Leuve ta grosse main
    diamante
Rende a rien les choses
    idiotique deboute,

Shit for the whores
    moronical of the devil—
Life is Not

Robert, Robert,
    I've lost you
    in the ocean of omniscience
    for ever
        already
            alas—!
The vines climb the posts,
Men suffer—
    The Buddhas
        sing tranquilly
        throughout all—
The sadness and the death
    and the false love
    of legs and tears—
Go out!—Come in!
Go up!   Run!
        Sleep!
Listen, Robert, the prayer
    of the Lord—for you—
"O Robert—who has the
    key of power
Raise your big hand
    of diamond.
        Bring to naught the things
        idiotically standing,

Detrui—
Extermine—
O Robert, donneur du
    courage, donne courage
    tous qu'ils sont
    en extremite de souffrance—
O Robert, qui Purifie,
    purifie tous qu'ils sont
    escalve d'l'ego
Que le victor de
    la souffrance, gagne—
    encore et encore—
O Robert, parfaitement
    en connaissance de
    la lumiere saint,
    amene toute les
    pauvres vivants de
    l'existence a ta
    connaissance.
O Robert, parfait en
    sagesse et amour
    tendre, sort toutes
    les pauvres vivants de
    leur prison d'existence
    et amene la a
        les Indes Sacrees
Om!   Amen!
Adoration a Tathagata
    le connaisseur de

Destroy—
Exterminate—
O Robert, giver of
  courage, give courage
  to all those who are
  in extremity of suffering—
O Robert, who Purifies,
  purify all who are
  slaves of the ego
May the victor of
  suffering, win—
  again and again—
O Robert, perfectly
  in consciousness
  of the holy light,
  bring all the
  poor living beings of
  existence to your
  consciousness.
O Robert, perfect in
  sageness and love
  tender, bring out all
  the poor living beings out of
  their prison of existence
  and bring them to
      the Sacred Nothingnesses
Om!   Amen!
Adoration to Tathagata
  the knower of

l'essence universelle
de toutes les choses
du reve et en dehors
du reve. A Sugata
le connaisseur de bonnesse
sans fin toupartout,
A Buddha, qui est
reveillez pour toujours
et a ete reveillez
pour toujours et sera
reveillez pour toujours,
parfait en pitie
et intelligence, qui
a accompli,
et accompli maintenant,
et accomplira, dans
toutes le directions vers
dedant et vers dehors,
toutes les mots de mystere."

Tire la manivelle
Amen
Par semaine.
A Dieu.
Bon Soir.
Un Bec.
Un nuee.
Adieu.

the Universal Essence
of all things
of the dream and outside
the dream. To Sugata
the knower of goodness
unlimited everywhere,
to Buddha, who is
awake for always
and has been awake
for always and will be
awake for always,
perfect in pity
and intelligence, who
has accomplished,
and accomplishes now,
and will accomplish, in
all directions in and out,
all the words of mystery."

Turn the handle.
Amen
By the week.
To God.
Goodnight.
A Kiss.
A cloud.
Farewell.

Autre foi.
Ma main.
Adieu.
Au Seigneur.
Bon Soir.
Dormez vous.

Ed: Kerouac didn't mark the French accents in his typescript of this poem, just
as he often ignored apostrophes in English.

Next time.
My hand.
Farewell.
To the Lord.
Goodnight.
Sleep you all.

October 10, 1955, Berkeley

GOD

In his jests serious, in his murders victim,
   or which, is God? Who began
   before non-existence's dependence
   on existence, Who came before
   the chicken and the egg

Who started out
              enormous Light
   the dark brilliance of the Mystery
   for all good hearts to shroud inside
   and keep their understanding sympathy
   intact as Beethoven's courageous
          slow sigh.

In his atrocities victim?
 In his jests damned?
 In his damnation damnation?
Or is God just the golden hover
   light manifesting Mayakaya
   the illusion of the moon, branches
   across the face of the moon?

O perturbing swttlontaggek
   montiana godio
 Thou high suffermaker!
Tell me now, in Your Poem!

HAIKU BERKELEY

Haiku Snyder
    I hurt the black ink
    on your kind book
  the only inconsistency sin
  I done yet to you
  sweet heart

And John Wino anyway
    was to blame

Dont kick me out
  of your tea
    house
  great man

Still a boy
Noble Youth
And when I meet you
Smash Mountain Man
A Million Ones from now
And offer you 5 Giant
           Flowers
And you predict me
         Tree Lover
  the Coming Lover

                    Buddha
                    of All the Worlds
                    With no body
                    & nothing distinguishable
                    from other bodies & yours
          By which time you'll be
          (you see) 6,000,000,000
                    years old
          I'll still call you Noble Youth,
             O Ever Weeping

                         *

Learned!   Learned!

This is the end
     of my enlightenment!

                         *

And you Whalen
   world slinger (like I said)
   Celt—
     You started it all
   And yr ideal eyes
   Blue love shining
   Everywhere
   Leave me never alone

                    44

For I whine
When otherwise
  Tryna be human

With no Buddha guts
& cant bend tendons
—O how collapsed
the tendon beam!—
Worms, a million years long
—Phillipi, shield,
 sun-star, wailer,
 Whalen, alright,
 excuse me for popping
              off

To hear the desert sigh

                    *

And you sweet Allen
  Ah Allen   Ah Me
    You know
      About me
        What I'd say
         Let it be
           We know
            We're old friends
& Never die

Lamantia Finally
Brilliant & Beautiful
What did you do?
(If I may ask a question)
With the golden rosary beads
I gave you 1955 years
           ago

                    *

I say "I'd like to see
The poems Li Po
Distributed in the Yellow River"
And Whalen says "Alright
We'll go down and dive
And see."

46

POIM

Walking on Water
Nothing Ever Happened
Not Ever Happening
True Story
Old Story
New Story
Old & New
HOLY BOLONEY
Holy Cow
Holy Cats
Wow
Whatever
To The Feast
Story Book
Book
Story Words
"Anyway, It Happened"
Nothing Happened
Everybody Invited

VARIOUS LITTLE POMES

The ants go roaming
in the mirror of
the mind,
over sand
which I see
falsely

*

I know this to be
an empty state,
that is to say,
a state of form

My dream of a
horrible city is
individual discrimination
—the actual
city is universal
mind

*

I stop dreaming
And the ripples
Disappear from
  universal mind's
    actual face
and what's left
  is I'm not here
any more

"Bodhisattva-Heroes have no separated individuality"

The reality is
nothingness—
We think
we strive

Primordially Undifferentiated

Sravasti, City of
Wonders, is now Village
of Sahet-Mahet,
River Rapti

*

Alone-one-All,
  I meditate Alone,
imitating Brahma
  God   Allah

TWO DHARMA NOTES

"The Buddha-Teaching
must be relinquished:
how much more so
misteaching."

   (Price's *Diamond Sutra*)

Mind Essence
(Tathagata-garbha)
is Non-Assertion
(Wu-Wei-Fa)

無
為
法

The
essence
is not
disturbed

"Unformulated
   Principle"

            *

51

7 treasures: gold,
silver, lapis lazuli,
cornelian, red pearls,
crystal, agate.

GATHA

Sitting in the chair
In the morning ground
Is no sitting in no
chair in no morning ground

No returning, no
   non-returning
No Karma, no
   non-Karma

"Happiness, abiding
in peace, in seclusion
in the midst of the
forest"
              is
  abiding nowhere

UnHappiness, abiding
  in anxiety in society
  in the midst of the
    city
              is
  abiding nowhere

Not-two,
          means,

no abider in his
    abode

No realizer in his
    realizing

"Develop a pure
  lucid mind"

              *

All things in the
River of Extinction
  already dead &
      extinct—
rocks, people,
    flowers—
even empty space
is extinct, since
it will have, has,
nothing to divide,
nothing to fill its
    empty form

The simplest fact
is that all things
die off—the
least fact faced
anywhere—
"All living beings
are not, in
fact, living beings"
because they're
dead in time—
time's a minute,
a pop—

No
time—Time is
extinct since it
will have, has, nothing
to change, nothing to fill
its empty form

*

54

At present, the
100,000,000th
myriad of multimillionth
Buddha is
    myself
  my-not-self

Thus　如

        (Tathagata,
        Arriver-at-Actual-Isness)

Come　來

This is my VYAKARANA Prediction
In the ages of the
future you will come to
be a Buddha called Smash
Mountain Man
(Gary Snyder)
In the ages of the future
I will come to be a
Buddha called Tree Lover
"Why predict the predictable?"

BEGINNING WITH A FEW HAIKUS
SOME OF THEM ADDRESSES IN THE BOOK

Lee Crawford
1126 San Benito
Burri Burri,
So. San Francisco
Calif.

F train
to University
& Shattuck
One block to left
(Ginsberg)

Snow Love

"Charming little bedraggled
princes"—Allen

1 HAIKU?

Disappointed in the
waning moon—
Pleiades, vine,
   wine bottle.

2

The waters see
The waters saw
So this is eternity

3

Can time crack rock?
  Marble'll chip,
  Diamond die.

4

Soup wont burn—
Spiders cant get
outa sinks—
Brew more tea

5

Mist in the window
Flower, weed,
Birds at dawn

6

Juju beads on
    Zen Manual—
My knees are cold

7

Morning, hot sun,
empty hard ground,
invisible voidness

8

Leaves dry Autumn
    yard,
Bed of white posies,
Spice bush sprouting

9

Flowers waiting,
Phantoms,
Phantasmal surface
of earth under
blue old space

10

NOT EVEN WORD FETTERED!
   NOT EVEN WAITING!
   NOT EVEN!

11 WALTER LEHRMAN'S HAIKU

One Friday when we were all dead
He said 'I didnt think it would
be so good.'

12

Dry old bigleaf,
   twisted young vine,
      pot with rag,
         million grasses
            shining

13 GARY SNYDER'S HAIKU *(Spoken on the Mountain)*

"Talking about the literary
life—the yellow
aspens."

14 GARY SNYDER'S SECOND HAIKU

"I get a hardon from here
to Connecticut, Goodness,
3,000 miles."

15 GARY SNYDER AGAIN

"I was thirteen
before I started skiing
during the war."

16 GARY AGAIN

"Just mad waiting for these
cocksucking letters—And
I go out to Central Park"

17 GARY AGAIN

"And there she is just an elegant—
And I'm wearing an old
pair of jeans"

18 GARY ONCE MORE

"There she is—I'm wearing
an old pair of jeans—
I say 'I've got to' "

19

Listen to the birds
sing!   All the little birds
will die!

20

Dusk: the bird on the fence
a contemporary
of mine

21

Nightfall: too dark
to read the page,
too cold.

22

Useless, useless,
heavy rain driving
into the sea!

23 GARY SNYDER

"Goofballs in the wine—
truck
goes by."

24

Drunk in the early morn
"Oooh" says my good
Buddha friend

25 HAIKU-KOAN

Does a dog have
the Buddha-nature?
Water is water.

26

You're bored.
Why?   I'm getting
to be old

27

First we buy the meat
and then we buy
the pot

28

There is no sin—
I know perfectly well
where I am

29

The Tathagata doesnt exist
in honor of which I will go
and climb mountains

30 GATHA

When I said to you
in Washington Square Park
"Am I my brother's keeper?"
it was Autumn

31 NATALIE'S HAIKU

"Remember that poet—
the girls are
talking now"

32 GARY

"Hundreds of comedies
about
aldultery"

33 HAIKU FROM A CARDBOARD BOX

Giant Tide
Gamble Made
   in America

34 GATHA

The world is old
   and wise
And I am tired
   of my eyes

35 GATHA

All kinds of young love
for sale
I cant get my black hands
on it

36

Decorated for the re-emergence
of the great
Virgin Fuck

37 PHILLIP WHALEN'S HAIKU

"Walked 5 miles with wine
then brought me
geranium"

[ENLIGHTENMENTS]

When you become enlightened
you will know that you've
been enlightened all along

*

Alright, I'm sick of this
enlightenment—now I'm
dumb again—the
delicate blue morning
sky thru the tree.

*

Dont worry about food,
Little John, there's some
  e v e r y w h e r e

*

Allen says "When people get
religious they start feeding
  e v e r y b o d y"

*

—The morning of
the end of my enlightenment

*

Enlightenment is: do what
    you want
   eat what there is

*

The soul burns out the eyes

World, it's about time you
realized there's too much food
for everybody to eat

*

The secret shape of the sun
Is a shield—flying to the right
To the West presumably
Just like the Roman Ear
Of Ezra Pound
In the Surrealist drawing
Just like Charioteer

*

The monument in the park
For the institute of the blind
Because it is not seen
Is truly a great monument

Would to God I could make one
So artistically fabulous
As that with my hands

*

Flowers aim crookedly
For the straight death

The white eyes of the criminals of Alcatraz thinking
thoughts of Love on their little Island Blest
while San Francisco crawls with hatred in the streets

And in rolls the Holy Fog from Jesus ballooning
Shrouds of puff over Gold's Gate—the mysterious
Source East of Western Torment, Western Me

*

Humility
  is
    Beatitude
    THE BEATIFIC GENERATION

*

Beginning to see the light, outside the church—
The Negro boy and the White boy
Hand in hand—Sunday morning with Philip Lamantia

*

There is the delusion of existence
because of my failure to realize
not-two-ness, i.e., deluded
and the deluding is the double
                    trick

Failure
            which is not really a failure
            really—
                        Ripple of delusion is
                            that it is

Con the train

                                *

There is gladness which the Saint feels;
there is mating, which the bitter husband feels;
but when gladness of mating is, is Love

BATH TUB THOUGHT

> A rock is like space
> because it doesnt move;
> And space is like a rock
> Because it is empty.
> Words are Buddhas.

*

Nothing's wrong
Something's right

W.C.Fields' Bathrobe

*

If I dont leave San Francisco
Soon—I'll be weeping cruds.
Wandering fair blossoms
        of false ethereality
        is what I see now.
Pretty soon I'll be down
On the Battered Internationale
Listening to devoured little girls
Who dance before the devout
And hungry men who devour
Her limb by limb, that
She's an artist
    Though clumsy
    Her big limbs move
    But she caint cackle
    Nor kick
        And nobody knows
        what to do
        with my woodshed
        blues.
    Goodbye, Rexroth
      until another time.

ON ETHER

Jordan Belson: "Everything is reduced
to its absolute meaning"

The Heel of Eloheim

Ether brings them out

*

Let slide sweetly
the transformations
of the thinking

*

The liberation
from Jack Kerouac

*

With Mike long ago
Under the little
dawn clouds—
waiting for the
work-car—Sebastian
was phenomenally
alive, is now
noumenally dead,
      just
        as
          pure
            as I

LETTER TO ALLEN 1955

I dont wanta see
  no Señora
De Hueva from Chappy
  Chi-a-pas—
Wot I got to do
  mit jungles?
And boogs? Malaria—
  Frogs, bulls, volcanoes,
  —

     hammocks of no rest
     hung in trees
     of antiquity
     full of moss
     and bacterii

Wanta go, I do,
  to sweet Watsonville,
  sleep in the river
  of Cairi

However, Garver and I
  do hereby formally
  request for Robert
  Lavigne's Mazatlan Address

MEXICO ROOFTOP

It's blue—with a pink movie neon
    E-changing in the jungle sky
    where rats havent chanced to swamp
    the mudstilt builders, but Who climbed,
    the builders, and made it the High Plateau

So's on October Fullmoon Nights, a palm
    hairs in the scene, and Aztec Temple
    apartment house arches stare
    with a premeditated ogling glare
    with light-holes & pool-puddles

And the dog barks at Stars—they
    are pretty quiet—Tho all kinds
    drams and whistlers hongkong the noise
    of the street the stars are as faint
    and as happy as they glow

In Sweet Canada or Carthage below,
    in Rome and in Sisyphus bosom
    —Urk, the brown strange glare
    of modernized Mexican architecture
    housingprojects cant be deAztecfied

It's blue—with day yellows night lemon
   and daywhites nightpale
   the color of chalk at a chalk quarry
   or gravel in hell—the walls
   of Jugurtha never as grim

I guess, as the walls of that side
   of the building—but music reforms
   the scene, atch or tortay, poor leetles
   Mexican lovers boys draining
   out their *corazon* for love of the sun

Awright, this poem's a failure—
Throw it in a drawer

MEXICAN LONELINESS

And I am an unhappy stranger
grooking in the streets of Mexico—
My friends have died on me, my
lovers disappeared, my whores banned,
my bed rocked and heaved by
earthquake—and no holy weed
 to get high by candlelight
 and dream—only fumes of buses,
dust storms, and maids peeking at me
 thru a hole in the door
 secretly drilled to watch
 masturbators fuck pillows—
 I am the Gargoyle
 of Our Lady
 dreaming in space
 gray mist dreams—
My face is pointed towards Napoleon
——I have no form——
My address book is full of RIP's
 I have no value in the void,
 at home without honor,—
My only friend is an old fag
 without a typewriter
Who, if he's my friend,
 I'll be buggered.

I have some mayonnaise left,
a whole unwanted bottle of oil,
peasants washing my sky light,
  a nut clearing his throat
  in the bathroom next to mine
  a hundred times a day
  sharing my common ceiling—
If I get drunk I get thirsty
—if I walk my foot breaks down
—if I smile my mask's a farce
—if I cry I'm just a child—
—if I remember I'm a liar
—if I write the writing's done—
—if I die the dying's over—
—if I live the dying's just begun—
—if I wait the waiting's longer
—if I go the going's gone—
if I sleep the bliss is heavy—
the bliss is heavy on my lids—
—if I go to cheap movies
     the bedbugs get me—
Expensive movies I cant afford
—If I do nothing
     nothing does

THE LAST HOTEL

The last hotel
I can see the black wall
I can see the silhouette in the window
He's talking
I'm not interested in what he's talking about
I'm only interested in the fact that it's the last hotel

The last hotel
Ghosts in my bed
The goats I bled
The last hotel

BERKELEY SONG IN F MAJOR

FAREWELL TO MY BABIES

Walt Whitman is striding
  Down the mountain of Berkeley
  Where with one step
  He abominates & destroys
  The whole atomic laboratory
  Wherein it becomes a jewel
  In his heel, O Eloheim!

With one quick look
  His belly golden bull
  He turns Mrs Matchyot
  To butter, one quick look
  Eats up the fairies & robbers
In Robbies coffee saloon,
  On he goes—wild hat
  Big white beard
  Fifteen feet tall
—No more lung stew
  "Why—Isnt he hungry?"
  "He eateth no more
  This is the final end—
He bears the 32 marks of perfection
He's on his way to Oakland
The cesspool of the Coast

Where beyond the dumps
I see telephone pole
A hundred miles high
With invisible wires
Of Transcendency—
Walt!   Jack!
Then across the Blue Bay
Gold step the Isle
Of Alcatraz, white eyes
Of lovely criminals,
Hatred Beaches, cops,
Pails, pockets, buckets,
Stores, sleeping bags,
Gold Gates & the Fog
Which Jesus Sendeth
from Up by Japan
the Alaskan Seal
Rock Territory
Known/ as Potato

(it all adds up to roil,
    or royal, one)
Walt Bluebeard Handsome
  Whitman, farewell
—For he also strides
  to East & gobbles
  Up Burma & Tits
  the Mock Top Peaks
  of T h i b e t a —

Returning, like sun
            the shield
Around the other side
Where first we thought
We saw him visioning
Down the shuddering mount
Of Berkeley's Atomic
Test Laboratory
Full of mice & men

—And it's snowing
This sunny morning

And the grass blade
   (so celebrate)
jostles slowly
      like a woman's
            beautiful
            breast
      side to side
In the Peep Show
   of Eternality
   & Salvation
      &
      and

S'nuf,—this parsimonious
pwap pwap tiddle
      all all day

We'll have no more jots & tittles
We'll have no more leaves
   broken off at the base
   of the Stem
  That means
   we'll have more jots & tittles
   more leaves like that
More
More gold
       & snow
       & show
But dont be fooled, kiddies—
The white screen is still
A White Screen
And the movie 'bout monkies
You see there
in the Vines & Berkelies
is projected by the spectral
  Honogrank Machine
  known as: Chaplin

Another name for film—
  T'all come from ether
  And t's'ether
  Either that or—What?
    Whop What But
     Bot Go On
      Bop Wallower?

Nay—
      Jack the middle
      Mass everything

          *

There's a tomato plant
In this mad garden of yrs
Allen Ginsberg
That grew six foot tall
And ran around along the
            high
            weed
With its empty-reed middle
The nature of which is as
            empty
            as
The sun that follows two guys
Walking away from the same
            poor
            pond
   And I seen the secret of the ant:
Which is:
  To them sand is boulders
  And the boulders are pure
            empty
            gold

Essence aint the ants
Essence aint Jack Whatyrcallit
Essence
Essence isnt a butter bee
                on a white petal
                dreaming of far
                 pure lands learned
                long ago
   Essence
   Essence, it means,
     Essence is the ants
     Is the Jack W i t t t
     Is the essence
     Is the long bee
          I told about

Is is
Is

A SUDDEN SKETCH POEM

Gary's sink has a shroudy burlap
  the rub brush tinware plout
     leans on right side
     like a red woman's hair
  the faucet leaks little lovedrops
The teacup's upsidedown with visions
  of green mountains and brown lousy
  Chinese mysterious up heights
  The frying pan's still wet
  The spoon's by 2 petals of flower
  The washrag's hung on edge like bloomers
  I dont know what to say
     about the dishpan, the soap
  The sink itself inside or what
  is hidden underneath the bomb burlap
Shroudflap except two onions
  And an orange and old wheat germ.
Wheat meal. The hoodlatch heliograph
With the cross that makes the devil
Hiss, ah, the upper coral sensen soups
  And fast condiments, curries, rices,
Roaches, reels, tin, tip, plastickets,
  Toothbrushes and armies, and armies
Of insulated schiller, squozen gumbrop

Peste pans, light of marin, pirshyar,
Magic dancing lights of gray and white
And all for verse I wrote it

April 1956, McCorkle's Shack

POEM WRITTEN IN THE ZOCO CHICO

He walks
  without thinking about the sea
His older brother
  shows his gold tooth
    trying to prove something on Sunday afternoon
One boy has a green fez
    that gives him permission from the sea
He's the *jamal* in the sea
that restores him harmlessly
He has any kinda claim
    to a gold chain
Some Burgher Berbers have false teeth
Then comes and overruns the great mock wave

  Some bulldogs have rubber teeth
The submarines are there to gyp the Egyptians
I see nothing there but a bird
The history of the world is lost in silence.

THREE TANGIER POEMS

Vapors mere
Shapes so dear?
Bell rung,
What's sung?

*

I strike at that snake-heart that hurt my family

*

Ah but Ah but Ah
   Where ocean water kisses beach sand
Lonely living blue balloon

The boys are kicking the ball
      far across the field—
The lonely goalie waits

What the Buddhas are saying
   in the "upper air":
Fish-film facing lost life-sea

My sweet spring sex loins
      joined to yours
Beneath the molten moon

TANGIER POEM

Your father spurted you out in perfect ghost-form

All you gotta do is die
All you gotta do is fly.
If your father's name is Dedalus
how can you be Icarus?

1957

POEM

Anyway the time has come to explain
    the Golden Eternity
and how the iridescent paraphernalia of radiating candles
    ceases
    when mentation ceases
because I know what it's like to die,
    to cease mentating, one day I died,
I fainted actually, I was stooping smelling
strapping flowers in the cosmos yard
of my mother's cozy flower house
in Auffinsham Shire, in Queens,
and stood up fast taking deep breath,
  blood rushed from head, next thing I knew
  woke up flat on my back in the grassy sun
  and had been out fine minutes.

And I had seen the Golden Eternity.
  The Lamb was alone with the Lamb.
  The Babe was alone with the Baby Lamb.
  The Shroud was alone with the Golden Shroud.

I was alone with God, who
  is God, who was Me,
  who was All,

he stood high on a hill
overlooking Mexico City
radiating messages
out of a white Tiot

1958, Northport

FLIES

And wasnt there ever a time when flies
  didnt seek the sun through forbidden
windowpanes?

And when men didnt pray for God
    to deliver them from mistake,
  Gesundheit?

Or when football players didnt huddle
    and plot the fall of opposing team
On chalkmark?

Who cares? God loves us all, his Own
    thought & Images in His dream,
Gesundheit.

No Jew of Torah or incantatory
    Koran was ever smarter
  than God.

Loved God—all love God, themselves
—why worry about the queer in Room 3?
God bless you.

Drink whisky sours in the Ritz
   at 3 pm Sunday talk of Tolstoy,
quien care?

   All I want outa this persephone
     is poems instructing lovemilk thru
anemone—

POEM

I could become a great grinning host
             like a skeleton

Hung Up In Heaven

HOW TO MEDITATE

       —lights out—
fall, hands a-clasped, into instantaneous
ecstasy like a shot of heroin or morphine,
the gland inside of my brain discharging
the good glad fluid (Holy Fluid) as
I hap-down and hold all my body parts
down to a deadstop trance—Healing
all my sicknesses—erasing all—not
even the shred of a "I-hope-you" or a
Loony Balloon left in it, but the mind
blank, serene, thoughtless. When a thought
comes a-springing from afar with its held-
forth figure of image, you spoof it out,
you spuff it off, you fake it, and
it fades, and thought never comes—and
with joy you realize for the first time
"Thinking's just like not thinking—
So I dont have to think
    any
   more"

BUDDHA

I used to sit under trees and meditate
on the diamond bright silence of darkness
and the bright look of diamonds in space
and space that was stiff with lights
and diamonds shot through, and silence

And when a dog barked I took it for soundwaves
and cars passing too, and once I heard
a jet-plane which I thought was a mosquito
in my heart, and once I saw salmon walls
of pink and roses, moving and ululating
with the drapish

Once I forgave dogs, and pitied men, sat
in the rain countin Juju beads, raindrops
are ecstasy, ecstasy is raindrops—birds
sleep when the trees are giving out light
in the night, rabbits sleep too, and dogs

I had a path that I followed thru piney woods
and a phosphorescent white hound-dog named Bob
who led me the way when the clouds covered
the stars, and then communicated to me
the sleepings of a loving dog enamoured
of God

On Saturday mornings I was there, in the sun,
contemplating the blue-bright air, as eyes
of Lone Rangers penetrated the dust
of my canyon thoughts, and Indians
and children, and movie shows

Or Saturday Morning in China when all is so fair
crystal imaginings of pristine lakes, talk
with rocks, walks with a Chi-pack across
Mongolias and silent temple rocks in valleys
of boulder and tarn-washed clay,—shh—
sit and otay

And if men were dyin or sleepin in rooftops
beyond, or frogs croaked once or thrice
to indicate supreme mystical majesty, what's
the diff? and I saw blue sky no different
from dead cat—and love and marriage

No different than mud—that's blood—
and lighted clay too—illuminated intelligent
faces of angels everywhere, with Dostoevsky's
unease praying in their X-brow faces,
twisted and great,

And many a time the Buddha played a leaf
on me at midnight thinkin-time, to
remind me 'This Thinking Has Stopped,'

which it had, because no thinking was there
but wasnt liquidly mysteriously brainly there

And finally I turned into a diamond stone
and sat rigid and golden, gold too—didnt dare
breathe, to break up the diamond that cant
even cut into butter anyway, how brittle
the diamond, how quick returned thought,—
Impossible to exist
     Buddha say:
    'All's possible'

POEM

I am God

HAIKU

Came down from my
  ivory tower
And found no world

MY VIEWS ON RELIGION

Heaven has everything to do with healing
and healing has nothing to do with heaven

If Jesus Christ is the son of God so am I

If suffering has anything to do
—if cake wont do, or cookies—
Heaven has everything to do with the way I feel
and I say *Heaven!* what you doin
down there, making like youse out
to beat hell—*Heaven!* How come

How come you got sixteen-year-old beauties
with lips parted open, in the moonlight
Italian balcony of me heart! *Heaven!*
Ope up them crazy open portal gates
and let the people pass, people pass

Revoke the Harrison Act! It is a Barbaric
act—It will cause desperate criminals
and gunmen to arise from our midst,
for evidential reasons—Ope nope—
It's like Prohibition, it wont, work,
—If the people want alcohol and dope
let em have alcohol and dope and all

101

the poison they can get if poison they want
—you cant tell the people what
to take in themselves—you cant stop
the people—I say this in the name of Peace
and I am not a Communist I'm a Dove

O ope them gordol golden gates

Buddha was not a medicine man,
he was a beyond-partition man,—
nor did he "limp for duty
             and crawl
        for charity"
             —*Chuangtse*

Buddha is God, the Father of Jesus Christ
AND GOD IS GOD

LADY

The universe is a lady
Holding within her the unborn light—
Our Lady, Nostre Dame.
It is fitting that Nostradamus could predict the future.
That is a function of our lady,
We the tealeaves.

CARITAS

Ah charity,—a little boy of eight or
seven, came up to sell little basket
flower candies in the teenage jukebox
soda saloon—nope, nobody buy—
and he walked barefoot in the rain

'Pas'd' Zapatas?' I think, No Shoes?
and I think 'I'll take out ten pesos
and give him for the shoes, say,
'Por usted, por tu zapatas'
and even show him how to hide the money

A sad song is playing, a harmonica,
as I first see his sad feet padding by
in the puddles of the sidewalk, O
the world is full of marvels—

Nostalgia, and I go after him to give
him his money, he goes into a huge
apartment house and there's the man
standing reading the floor-numbers
quietly, as little boy waits, both facing me

that's across the street with money in hand,
both stare, movingless, wait, the drape falls,

Aztec shrouds her mystery, & up they go
as grawmim elevator door closes
on both their heavenly chagrins

I think "Is he gone up there, he lives
up there with his folks and sells bonbons
barefoot, or is just hitting the joint
door to door to sell among the government
employee families of Childe Mexico"

And think "And it was said in the
Diamond Sutra so holy and so high,
practice generosity without entertaining
in mind any limited conceptions of the
reality of the feeling of generosity, or

what'll it accomplish for you, pard,
this is the word from old Buddha-hard
and he's spoken by a diamond tree,
and thousands-a people go barefoot,
it's written in every hemisphere

              song of every sphere

Song of every sphere from every Child Revere
—Song of any morning waters blue with dream
by the broken Coney Island Staten statue
with no Medusa Snakehead arms and
no stone afoot, O Marva my foot

And we drive along in an insane dream
with our mouths distorted and eyes gleaming
crookedly every way, driving by iron rusty
steerages belonging to Babylonian Old
Zapoteca Arabian Neolithic
apathetic

old somervance, prance, hand me the foot,
we come di-vowing down the planks
and hit the water's admirable edge
and there's a tent and Side-Show
that I go to, to see girls

POEM

Old hornet me
Would woo thee
Fair, soft Sara
Of the flowers;
But bee's not kind
That seeks to find,
Peers too deep
Shares no sleep;
And anyway,
Who woos bees?

LIL POEM ON LOUIS FERDINAND CÉLINE

Where the madman plays with his fertilizers,
Where the mad priest comes in the window covered with mud,
Where the submarine knocks down the walls of the publisher,
Céline, Céline, Céline.

SKID ROW WINE

I coulda done a lot worse than sit
in Skid Row drinkin wine

To know that nothing matters after all
To know there's no real difference
between the rich and the poor
To know that eternity is neither drunk
nor sober, to know it young
and be a poet

Coulda gone into business and ranted
And believed that God was concerned

Instead I squatted in lonesome alleys
And nobody saw me, just my bottle
and what they saw of it was empty

And I did it in cornfields & graveyards

To know that the dead dont make noise
To know that the cornstalks talk (among
one another with raspy old arms)

Sittin in alleys diggin the neons
And watching cathedral custodians
Wring out their rags neath the church steps

Sittin and drinkin wine
And in railyards being divine

To be a millionaire & yet to prefer
Curlin up with a poorboy of tokay
In a warehouse door, facing long sunsets
On railroad fields of grass

To know that the sleepers in the river
are dreaming vain dreams, to squat
in the night and know it well

To be dark solitary eye-nerve watcher
of the world's whirling diamond

THE MOON

The moon her magic be, big sad face
Of infinity   An illuminated clay ball
Manifesting many gentlemanly remarks

She kicks a star, clouds foregather
In Scimitar shape, to round her
Cradle out, upsidedown any old time

You can also let the moon fool you
With imaginary orange-balls
Of blazing imaginary light in fright

As eyeballs, hurt & foregathered,
Wink to the wince of the seeing
Of a little sprightly otay

Which projects spikes of light
Out the round smooth blue balloon
Ball full of mountains and moons

Deep as the ocean, high as the moon,
Low as the lowliest river lagoon
Fish in the Tar and pull in the Spar

Billy de Bud and Hanshan Emperor
And all wall moongazers since
Daniel Machree, Yeats see

Gaze at the moon ocean marking
the face—

        In some cases
        The moon is you

        In any case
        The moon

POEM

Told him all about Minoan Civilization
   in front of Father Duffy's statue
      Told him all about
      Minoan Civilization
In Father Duffy's statue
Told him all about portals
Gotta be holy high

THE THRASHING DOVES

In the back of the dark Chinese store
   in a wooden jailhouse bibbet box,
   with dust of hay on the floor, rice
   where the rice bags are leaned,
   beyond the doomed peekokoos in the box
   cage

All the little doves'll die.
   As well as the Peekotoos—eels
   —they'll bend chickens' necks back
   oer barrels and slice at Samsara
   the world of eternal suffering with silver
   blades as thin as the ice in Peking

As thick & penetrable as the Wall of China
   the rice darkness of that store, beans,
   tea, boxes of dried fish, doodlebones,
   pieces of sea-weed, dry, pieces of eight,
   all the balloon of the shroud on the floor

And the lights from little tinkly Washington St.
   Behung, dim, opium pipes and gong wars,
   Tong, the rice and the card game—and
   Tibbet de tibbet the tink tink tink
   them Chinese cooks do in the kitchen
   Jazz

The thrashing doves in the dark, white fear,
   my eyes reflect that liquidly
   and I no understand Buddha-fear?
   awakener's fear? So I give warnings
   'bout midnight round about midnight

And tell all the children the little otay
   story of magic, multiple madness, maya
   otay, magic tree-sitters and little girl
   bitters, and littlest lil brothers
   in crib made of clay (blue in the moon).

For the doves.

THE SEA-SHROUD

The Sea-Shroud comes out of a slip
  of water in Brooklyn Harbor, night,
  it emerges from a submerged tug
  right from the enamel underwear
  of the pilot's cabin

Right through up comes the shroud head,
  a draining drape of wet weedy
  watery sea net spray, ephemeral,
  climbing to knock knees against the bow
  and make the bit on the dock

And come on vanishing instead
  reappearing as a Man
  with a briefcase, on Borough Hall,
  saying nothing with a watery face
  saying nothing with an ogoo mouth

Saying nothing with a listening nose,
  saying nothing with a questionmark mouth,
  saying nothing, the briefcase full
  of seaweed—what happens to floating
  bonds when they get in the hand of the drape

115

Sea-shroud, turning Chinese Food to seaweed
    in his all-abominable bag, Shroud
    the taker of widows' monies in red allies
    of shame & stagedoors, purple lagoon,
    Goon Shroud departs gloving the money

Earlier in the day he'd perched atop a
    flagpole in a parking lot
    on the waterfront, and looked around
    to see which way Borough Hall
    which way the little white doves

MY GANG

I

Many people have been frighted & died in cemeteries
   since the days of my gang, the night
   Ninip Houde came up & talked to me
   on the block and I rowed the imaginary
   horse on the rowel of the porch rail

Where I killed 700,000 flies or more
   while Ma and Beatrice gossiped
   in the kitchen, and while drape sheets
   we airing on the line that's connected
   to midnight by midnight riding roses

Oy—the one bad time that Zaggo
   got home from school late, dark
   in the streets, the sisters majestico
   blooming in the alley retreat, beat,
   'Your gang is upstairs' says my mother

And I go up to my closed smoky door
   and open it to a miniature poolhall
   where all the gang is smoking & yakking
   with little cue sticks and blue chalk
   around a miniature table on stilts

Bets being made, spittings out the window,
    cold out there, old murder magoon
    the winter man in my tree has seen
    to it that inhalator autumn
    prestidigitate on time & in ripe form,
    to wit cold

To wit cold, to wit you, to wit winter
To wit time, to wit bird, to wit dust—
  That was some game ole Salvey blanged
  When he beat G.J. that time,
    and Rondeau roared

II

Rondeau was the cookie that was always
    in my hair, a ripe screaming tight
    brother with heinous helling neck-veins
    who liked to riddle my fantasms
    with yaks of mocksqueak joy

"Why dont you like young Rondeau?"
    always I'm asked, because he boasts
    and boasts, brags, brags, ya, ya, ya,
    because he's crazy because he's mad
    and because he never gives us a chance to talk

Awright—I'd like to know what
Bobby's got against me—But he wont
tell, and it's brother deep—In the room
they're shooting the break, clack,
the little balls break, scatter di mania,

They take aim on little balls and break
    em up to fall, in plicky pockpockets
    for little children's names drawing
    pictures in the games in the whistle
    of the old corant tree splashing

In the mighty mu Missouri lame image
    of time and again the bride & groom,
    boom & again the bidal bood, oo,
    too-too and rumble o mumble thunder
    bow, ole Salvey is in my alley

Ole Salvey's my alley I'll lay it on me
    I'll shoot fourteen farthings for Father Machree
    and if ole Hotsatots dont footsie
    down here bring my gruel, I'll
    be cruel, I'll be cruel

PAX

I demand that the human race
ceases multiplying its kind
    and bow out
    I advise it

And as punishment & reward
for making this plea I know
    I'll be reborn
    the last human

Everybody else dead and I'm
an old woman roaming the earth
    groaning in caves
    sleeping on mats

And sometimes I'll cackle, sometimes
pray, sometimes cry, eat & cook
    at my little stove
    in the corner
  "Always knew it anyway,"
      I'll say
And one morning wont get up from my mat

HAIKU

The moon,
   the falling star—
Look elsewhere

PRAYER

O Lord, what have you hoarded up
   for me
In your great free treasure?

POEM

You start off by suckin in
   milk
And you end up suckin in
   smoke

And you know
What milk and smoke
Denote

ANGEL MINE

Angel mine be you fine
Angel divine

Angel milk what's your ilk
Angel bilk

Angel cash   Angel Smash
Angel hash

PERM

The world goes on
The junkey drops his butt
Children yell 'Hallelujah
    praise God!'
in the streets of sorrow parade

POEMS OF THE BUDDHAS OF OLD

by Jean-Louis

I

The boys were sittin
In a grove of trees
Listenin to Buddy
Explainin the keys.

"Boys, I say the keys
Cause there's lots a keys
But only one door,
One hive for the bees.

So listen to me
And I'll try to tell all
As I heard it long ago
In the Pure Land Hall.

Life is like a dream,
You only think it's real
Cause you're born a sucker
For that kind of deal;

But if the Truth was known
You ain't here nohow

And neither am I
Nor that cow and sow

You see across the field
One standing silently
The other rutting ragefully
In essence so quietly.

For you good boys
With winesoaked teeth
That can't understand
These words on a heath

I'll make it simpler
Like a bottle a wine
And a good woodfire
Under the stars divine.

Now listen to me
And when you have learned
The Dharma of the Buddhas
Of old and yearned

To sit down with the truth
Under a lonesome tree
In Yuma Arizony
Or anywhere you might be

Don't thank me for telling
What was told me,
This is the Wheel I'm turning,
This is the reason I be.

Mind is the maker
For no reason at all
Of all this creation
Created to fall.

II

"Who played this cruel joke
On bloke after bloke
Packing like a rat
Across the desert flat?"

Asked Montana Slim
Gesturing to him
The buddy of the men
In this lion's den.

"Was it God got mad
Like the Indian cad
Who was only a giver
Crooked like the river?

Gave you a garden,
Let the fruit harden,
Then comes the flood
And the loss of your blood?

Pray tell us, good buddy
And don't make it muddy
Who played this trick
On Harry and Dick

And why is so mean
The Eternal scene,
Just what's the point
Of this whole joint?"

III

Replied the good buddy:
"So now the bird's asleep
And that air plane gone
Let's all listen deep.

Everybody silent
Includin me
To catch the roar
Of eternity

That's ringin in our ears
Never-endingly.
You hear it Tom, Dick
And Harry Lee?

You hear it Slim
From Old Montan'?
You hear it Big Daddy
And Raggedy Dan?

You know what I mean
When I say eternity?
You heard it in your crib—
Shhh—Infinity."

IV

Up spoke Big Daddy
From Baltimore
An enormous Negro
Forevermore:

"You mean that shushin
And that fussin
A-slushin in my ears
For all these years?

When I was so high
Jess a little guy
I thought it was me
In the whisperin sea.

I asked my Mam
About that jam,
She didn't say nothin,
She sewed the button.

It was quiet and late
At the afternoon grate.
Her face showed no sign
Of that whisperin line

But as we sat waitin
Instead of abatin
The noise got to roar
Like an openin door

That opened my haid
Like if it was daid
And the only thing alive
Was that boomin jive

And we looked at each other
Child and mother
Like wakin from a dream
In a spirit stream."

V

"Well spoken, Big Daddy!"
Cried the buddy real glad.
"This proves that you know
And you'll never be sad.

For that was the sound
That we all hear now
And I want you to know
It's no sound nohow

But the absence of sound
Clear and pure,
The silence now heard
In heaven for sure.

What's heaven?
By Nirvana mean I?
This selfsame no-sound
Silence sigh

Eternal and empty
Of sounds and things
And all thievin rivers
Complainin brings.

For if we can sit here
In this riverbottom sand

And come to see
And understand

That we got in us
Ability to hear
Holy Emptiness
Beyond the ear

And block our ears
And hear inside
And know t'aint here
Nor there, the tide,

But everywhere, inside,
Outside, all throughout
Mind's dream, Slim?
What you gripin about?

Imaginary rivers
And gardens too,
A movie in the mind
Of me and you.

The point
Of this whole joint
Is stop, sit,
And thee anoint

With teachings such
As these, and more,
To find the key
Out this dark corridor.

The effulgent door,
The mysterious knob,
The bright room gained
Is the only job."

             The boys was pleased
             And rested up for more
             And Jack cooked mush
             In honor of the Door.

MORPHINE

The magic instance of the parriot tree
Nothing like a shot of junk for sheer
Heavenly contact
Oh yah, clear as a bell the mind
On morphine

I got all eternity to do everything
    you want me to do
So there's no rush

SILLY GOOFBALL POMES

SONG OF THE NEW CHINESE

I

The Moose is a noble dolt.
  The Elk is a fool.
  The Rhinoceros is the biggest bore
          of them all.
  The Hippopotamus is a Giant River Pig.
  The Hyena is a striped dog
      who thought he was a Laughing Horse.
  The Lion is a Queer Cat
      who by the Power of his Queerness
      became a great jowled Cat.
  The Tiger is pure cat.
  The Panther hates cats.
  The Cheetah is a dog
      who thought he was a Fast Cat.
The Giraffe is a Horse
      who grew fond of Tree-Top Leaves.
The Snake has a body beautiful,
  And the Elephant is the Lord,
          the Hook & Curl of his trunk,
          the long-lashéd Eye.
The Sloth is a Chinese Poet upsidedown.

The Ant-Eater is a long-nosed
    investigator of Villages.
The Scorpion is a Sea-Spider trapped
            on land.
The Whale is More so.
  The Man is very strange.

II

The Spider monkey is a little fool.
  The Pekinese Doll is a dog.
    The Dachshund is a snake full of Love.
    The Siamese Cat is an Angry Monkey.
      The Woman is a cellular mesh of lies
          as well as a Scratcher.
      The Woman has a dark blossom
              between her Thighs.
The Buddha is Known.
  The Messiah is Unborn.
The Boll Weevil is a pants rotter.
The ant a Warrior.
    The worm is a long history
          oozing out of Who?
  Who!
  Mu!
  Wu!
    The dog is a god.
    The dog is a balker.

The Leopard is Incontinent, said Dante,
    free from the Severity of Leopard.
The Angel Rules the Jungle.
 Blake is Blake.
The Cow has its own way with water.
And the Tick sticks in your hair
   & swells—
The Shark I never Saw

The purple ass baboon is Insane
The Sparrow is a little grey bird
The Chimpanzee is Wise
The American a Sniper
The Gull a bringer of Snail Shells
The Parrot I love
 The snail knows the Unborn Void
   of Tao
    and that's why he left his house
    for Gull
 The Sea Bird is all Belly
Crows are Dawn Singers
 The Bee hums busily
   The Frog leaped out of Water
    The Abominable Snowman is not abominable at all,
    he doesnt hurt anybody—
   The Rat has many theories—
   The Spider means money—
   The Fly has Seven Million
     brothers—

The Seal
is on my Roof

The Goose goes north
The Robin wins the spring
The caterpillar waits
The Nightingale I have been
The mockingbird loves TV aerials
The Rabbit
The vulture trails the Puma
  The wolf snaps the Bear
    The Lizard
     The Eel
       The Octopus
        The Tapeworm
        The Finger
         The Cock
           The Germ
             The Fingernail
             The Wall

The Swordfish has a Beak of Wood.
  The Lobster is friendly.
    The Flea leaps,
      The Cockroach is Reverenced,
        The Bedbug rolls.

POME

Be me bespangled dotted-hat fool?
  Jump upsidedown Pandora? leap above?
   —make burping Kings laugh for Ide?
—remember?—
     I'd rather piss on Scroll
than parch this

3 POEMS ABOUT
TITLES OF NOVELS

White Story
Story in White
  Never Be Mean
Some Ending
  No Red Eye in Heaven
  White Legs
          A Few Years
        More Boloney
      More of the Same
      Rest and Be Kind
          Kindness is All
          All One Way
          To Heaven
          Only Looking
            Story
            A Story
          Book Movie
        Story in Words
          Story Line

          *

Words Cawn't Tell
Holy Violinists
Violin
Rabbit Violin
There's a Rabbit in Heaven
One Means Not Two
One
One, Not Two
Not Two
Three
Thirty Three
Eleven
Seven Times Seven
Seven come Eleven
Seventy Seven

Follow the Lamb
Follow
Heaven Followed
Heaven Follows

*

Plenty Room in the Inn
Bright Room
  Plenty Room
Sheol
  Gadster

Bing Bang
            Ding Dong
Bing Bong
Dreamers Alive

No Title
Not Even
Never
No
Quack Quack
Pa Drift

TO LOU LITTLE

Lou, my father thought you put him down
  and said he didnt like you

He thought he was too shabby for your
  office; his coat had got so

And his hair he'd comb and come
  into an employment office with me

And have me speak alone with the man
  for the two of us, then sigh

And repented we home; where
  sweet mother put out the pie

       anyway

In my first game I ran like mad
  at Rutgers, Cliff wasnt there;

He didnt believe what he read
  in the Spectator, 'Who's this Jack?'

So I come in on the St Benedicts game
  not willing to be caught by them bums

I took off the kickoff right straight at
    the gang, and lalooza'd around

To the pastafazoola five yard line,
    you were there, you remember

We didnt make first down; and I
    took the punt and broke my leg

And never said anything, and ate hot
    fudge sundaes & steaks in the
            Lion's Den

AIRAPETIANZ

Airapetianz, that's his name, connected
with the invention of brainwashing, if
not the inventor himself, a Pavlovian
issue taking place in science whereas
ulcer patients feel no pain
   but mind pain

As outside chloroformeters take in
the reading of the pain sensation,
and prove there is no body pain,
inside his mind he's struggling with numbers
that tell him he's alright or not

Drinks that in, that info, and registers
no body pain—Suddenly it reads *5!*
it means he's having an attack!
Immediately the meter goes up (in
his mind) but on the board no reading
   is made

Because pain sensation not coming in

So Airapetianz proves that pain
   has mental sources

Mind over matter and mind over pain

Pavlovian instrument, determinism
And brainwash it's called

      Which doesnt matter
      In a mindmatter world
      The dog that barks
      The wick that falls
      The soul that goes to heaven
      The hand that writes

IF I WERE JESUS, GOD

O tender hearted sweet usurper of my
   vines, fox, do not crawl too near

O marblehearted faun of antiquity,
   what can I say of thee?

O people of Carthage! Oh Rome!
O Northside Chicaga! O Tome!

O listen to me in the park—
     Whenever you have a question
     come to me

Otherwise I'll be in the Tree Grove
   resting up

IDIOT

Them Hindu temples in Hoopastan
Hoo! them Hindu temples'd a made
Fool! outa me if I laffed like that
Hyah! hyah hyoo hya hya hoo-a
Thee! marvelous parvelous pairvening
Raive! ening of this ard-parturying-
Spring?—they give it that name in Ego's
Ed! cave, in Spatn, latn, you know,
Piss! tayola manaya tapaya you
Know! ho!—the lark's fat frant
Mar!—jesty hit the seapebble Homeric
Good!—fragrance I descried in gulls'
Art! fly majesty, known as then mad,
Read! Sherwood's Anderson Ohio Ville
Story! of epic O hand,—Yippee!
Yell! the Madman in the next room
Amazed! the doctor with a crazed
Jump? in the air, *I'm* mad?

> Well I only said
> You were an idiot

Idiots have Kings, were Kings, have necks
to be cut off, gibbets to spin rope of,
Twisted pants to sweep blond hair

Of HomoSexual Heroes testifying testes
In courts of Conelrad Behavious otay—
        Otay!

   Sneak out of it with jazz

Hey! Ole Idiot's still on the corner
Ready for all comers

OLD WESTERN MOVIES

A Jedge in the West comin from the South
   with ruby sideburns, boy—
Always usin flowery languij—
The grim fightin hero's troubles
   are always private—
He wants to know where "I fit in"
   in herd wars—
Sometimes you see villains so ancient
  you saw them in infancy
  exaggerating in snow
their mustaches looking older
    than yr father's grave—
"Thanks Marshall"—"I reckon"
—I guess I better run on back
   to Whisky Row, Colorada,
   & marry an old Tim McCoy Gal
   or turn off the tele vision, *one*—

—You gotta go a long way in the West
     to find a good man—
  So close the book,
  The Courier, run by Steve, is a paper
  wearing a sunbonnet.
  Drive the cattle thru that silver wall,
      help ladies to their hearse,
          mouth in the sun,

That oughta do till Mexican Drygulcher
   finds Redwing in the Shack
 And Kwakiutls menstruate.
Old horses' necks by broken fences,
   guns gone rust,
I guess the gang got shot.

     Kid Dream
    Hid
     In the leaves.

April 1958, Northport

WOMAN

A woman is beautiful
 but
     you have to swing
     and swing and swing
     and swing like
     a handkerchief in the
                wind

HYMN

And when you showed me Brooklyn Bridge
  in the morning,
    Ah God,

And the people slipping on ice in the street,
twice,
    twice,
        two different people
        came over, goin to work,
        so earnest and tryful,
        clutching their pitiful
        morning Daily News
        slip on the ice & fall
        both inside 5 minutes
        and I cried I cried

That's when you taught me tears, Ah
  God in the morning,
    Ah Thee

And me leaning on the lamppost wiping
eyes,
    eyes,
        nobody's know I'd cried
        or woulda cared anyway

151

but O I saw my father
and my grandfather's mother
and the long lines of chairs
and tear-sitters and dead,
Ah me, I knew God You
had better plans than that

So whatever plan you have for me
Splitter of majesty
Make it short
  brief
Make it snappy
  bring me home to the Eternal Mother
  today

At your service anyway,
  (and until)

GOOFBALL BLUES

I'm just a human being with a lot of
shit on my heart

My ambition was not to be a great
lover,
but that's what I am
Even in dreams, fiancées
of other men
ball on my joint
And I am the Flying Horse
of Mien Mo
When I am an old man
my grave will rot me
The ones I loved were crazy
without knowing why
When I am old I'll yawn
in the Flannel Grave

GOOFBALL SILLYPOMES

These Englishers know more madness
Than Nonsense Poems know,
For Tom O' Bedlam never dreamed
What's dream'd in mattress now,
        Enow, M.J.E.,
            Enow

Those who die
  go to coffins
That never get wet

The old years
  on the dock
—Blue air

The wind is late
—Already this gate
Has not been swept

Jan, 1960

DRUNKEN SCRIBBLING POEM

I got no language left in me heart
I'm a triple trombone fool
The Three Vehicles are a drag on my ass

Ah Sad America your cluster of girlies—All of a High School
afternoon waiting for the bass drum Master with his Golden Fish
Pole "Hike!" he yells "Realize!" dont amble just bramble in my
flying airplane bushes with me dont let ornery old hometown
friends in cars go C' cree-acking (Runnin Wild) yair, go ahead
home is soon—If my own kid did true be damned hummmmmm
into each rain the right rain poured ahh and go blue you River
Yair reaning calling more   O   Rooder   you downed yair Oh
Yess Og nobody tree ah alone they aint nobody home
          Figure that out if you will, Drop
          Milton is back
          Dread dread dread dread dread dread is dead   oh
the sorrowful twap of that tirler
          Let no honest (let no oneset englishman) twirl
          Onest

1959, Northport

155

RUNNING THROUGH—
CHINESE POEM SONG

O I today
sad as Chu Yuan
stumbled to the store
in broiling Florida October
morning heat cursing
for my wine, sweating
like rain, & came to my chair
weak & trembling
wondering if I'm crazy at last
—O Chu Yuan! No!
No suicide! Wine please wine!
What shall we all do
all knowing we're dying
without wine to guide us
to winking at death
& life too——
My heart belongs
to Chinese poets
& their scrolls—
We cant just die
—Men need wine
& poetry
at least

O Mao, poet Mao,
not Boss Mao,
here in America
wine is laughed at
& poetry a joke
—Death's a grim reminder
to everybody already dead
crashing in cars all around here—
Here men & women dryly scowl
at poets' sad attempts
to make our lot
a whole lot
lesser—
I, a poet, suffer
even for bugs
I find upsidedown
dying in the grass—
So I drink wine
alone—
I shudder to think
how dead
the astronauts
are
going to a dead
moon
of no wine

All our best men
are laughed at
in this nightmare land
but the newspapers preen
in virtue—Throughout
the world the left & right,
the east & west, are both vicious—
The happy old winebibber is gone—
I want him to reappear—
For Modern China preens
in virtue too
for no better reason
than America—
Nobody has respect for the cat
asleep, and I am hopelessly
inadequate in this poem
—Nobody has respect
for the self centered
irresponsible wine invalid
—Everybody wants to be strapped
in a hopeless space suit
where they cant move
—I urge you, China,
go back
to Li Po &
Tao Yuan Ming

What am I talking about?
I dont know,
   I'm sick today—
I didnt sleep all night,
Walked stumbling in the field
  to get wine, now I'm drinking it,
  I feel better and worse—
  I have something to say to Mao
  & the poets of China
     that wont come out—
     It's all about how America
     ignores poetry & wine,
     & so does China,
        & I'm a fool
           without a river & a boat
           & a flower suit—
           without a wineshop at dawn
           ——without self respect—
              —

        —Without the truth—
        but I'm a better man
        than all of you—
           that's what I
           wanted to say

1961

159

SKEN 3

Radiations of Akshobya
Blinding my eye in the
 water in the claypot
 pan-pot, the rainbow
 of the sun's reflection
 there causing painful
 imaginary blossoms to
 arise in my eyeball
and I see silver daggers
 & swords mingled with
 red or rather roe-pink
 rowing fires, shot by
 quivers & Arch Bows of
 Tampleton Hokshaw
 HighRide Chariot Ear
 the saint of England,
 Wozzit, turning pools
 of oil rainbow Dedalus
—Buddhalands without
 number & Van Gogh swirl
 agog rows of em endless
 emptiness in that little
 pot, & bug flies—

COGNAC BLUES

You gets your just dues in
Heaven——Heaven'll
be indifferent to this
indifferent dog

(Yet, honest indifference
were better than cant)

. . . really

When I hear pious
bullshit about Justice
& Democracy and I know
the hypocrites are lying
in their false teeth

I'm not indifferent to God,
I'm indifferent to
me-on-earth

I cant think of anything
more ridiculous than me
on earth—
Really!

BEAU BÉBÉ

And the dreams—of me & Lousy & GJ
   sitting on Moody St looking up the
   bridge to P'Ville where vistas
      of vast sunny cloud boulevard
      Buddhalands open, I tell
      Lousy "This is a dream"—
      big rivers, lake————
      I tell Lousy that, he gives
      me the thin Kasyapa's Smile—
      GJ too bored to comment—
   ————Like holding up a flower,
   as Ma says: "The Beginning"—
Later after being jacked off in
      the NY subway by stealer
      blondes with pimps in background
   (Ah the Ecstasy) I
      stole over well remembered
      other-people roofs—

1961, Orlando, Fla.

THE SHACK OF DESOLATION

The shack of Desolation is dirty, with broken boxes of wood
    gathered by me like a Japanese old woman gathers
    driftwood on the beach or on the mountainside,

Full of mice, fat drops, chips, ancient chewed up fragments
    of religious tracts, crap, dust, old letters of other lookouts
    and general unsweepable debris too infinitude to assemble
    and sweep

Paniaw Powder   Olympic   Pawmanow

And Mt Hozomeen—most beautiful mountain I ever seen—
    frights me acme out the morning coffee window,
    blue Chinese void of Friday morning,

And I have an old washtub covered with a wood door of sheds
    that when I saw it made me think of oldtime baths
    of bathnight New England when Pa was pink—

    Patiat rock mounts snow spomona'd that I drew at ten
    for Kuku and Coco everywhere, hundreds a miles of,
    and clouds pass thru my ink

POOR SOTTISH KEROUAC

Poor sottish Kerouac with his thumb in his eye
Getting interested in literature again
Though a mote of dust just flew by

How should I know that the dead were born?
Does Master cry?

   The weeds Ophelia wound with
      and Chatterton measured in the moon
      are the weeds of Goethe, Wang Wei,
        and the Golden Courtesans

Imagining recommending a prefecture
      for a man in the madhouse
          ——rain——

  Sleep well, my angel
  Make some eggs
  The house in the moor
  Is the house in the moor
  The house is a monument
  In the moor of the grave
  ——Whatever that means——

   The white dove descended in disguise?

LONG ISLAND CHINESE POEM RAIN

The years are hurrying
Autumn rains fall on my awning
My accomplishments mean nothing to me
My girl no longer visits me

Maybe because I got warts on my cock
Or she found a younger man with a smooth cock
I can look up anything in my wine bottle

Whitman was happy about something around here
  Followed by millions sick
What, Whitman, say?

The headlines of ten days ago no longer interest me
Rugs woven lovingly end on garage crates

The white dove desecrated in desuetude
And who wants wisdom?

The world is an eraser for these words

Oh sad Bodhidharma you were right
Everything we loved disappeared

Nobody in the chair
Nobody in the books
Nobody in the rain

1961

POME

If I dont use the cork
I may spill the wine—
But if I do?

POME ON DOCTOR SAX

In his declining years Doctor Sax was an old bum living in Skid
Row hotel rooms in the blighted area of SF around 3rd
Street—He was a madhaired old genius now with hair
growing out of his nose, like the hair growing out of
the nose of Aristadamis Kaldis the painter, and had
eyebrows growing out an inch long, like the eyebrows
of Daisetz Suzuki the Zen Master of whom
it has been said, of *which*, eyebrows like that
take a lifetime to grow so long &
therefore resemble the bush of the
Dharma which once rooted
is too tough to be
pulled out by hand
or horse—

Let that be a lesson to all you young
girls plucking your eyebrows & you
(also) young choir singers jacking off
behind the marechal's hilt
in St Paul's
Cathedral
(& yelling home to Mother
"Mater Mine, b'ome
for Easter")

Dr Sax the master knower of
 Easter was now reduced to penury
    & looking at Stained glass windows
    in old churches—His only 2
    last friends in this life, this impossibly
      hard life no matter under what
    conditions it appears, were Bela
    Lugosi & Boris Karloff, who visited
him annually in his room on 3rd Street
    & cut thru the fogs of evening with
    their heads bent as the bells of St Simon
    tolled a heartbroken "Kathleen" across
    the rooftops of old hotels where similar old
    men like Doctor Sax sat bent headed
    on beds of woe with prayerbeads between
       their feet, Oh moaning, homes for
            lost pigeons or time's immemorial
                white dove
                  of the roses
                    of the unborn
                      astonished bliss—

   And there they'd sit in the little
 room, Sax on the edge of the bed with a
 bottle of rotgut Tokay in his hand, Bela
 in the old rocking chair, Boris standing by
            the sink, & sigh————
              & then Sax wd always say

"Please play the monster for me" & of course
the old actors, who loved him dearly & came to
see him for human tender sentimentality not
monstrous reasons protested but he always
got drunk & cried so that Boris first had
to get up & extend his arms do
Frankenstein go *uck!* then Bela
wd stand & arm cape & leer &
approach Sax, who squealed

1961

A CURSE AT THE DEVIL

For Charleen Whisnant

Lucifer Sansfoi
  Varlet Sansfoi

Omer Perdieu
  I.B.Perdie
  Billy Perdy

I'll unwind your
  guts from Durham
    to Dover
    and bury em
    in Clover—

Your psalms I'll 'ave
  engraved
    in your toothbone—

Your victories
nilled—
You jailed under
a woman's skirt
  of stone—

Stone blind woman
with no guts
and only a scale—

Your thoughts & letters
Shandy'd about
    in *Beth*
      (Gaelic for *grave*).

Your philosophies
run up your nose
again—

Your confidences
and essays bandied
  in ballrooms
from switchblade
  to switchblade

—Your final
duel with
  sledge hammers—
Your essential
secret twinned
  to buttercups
    & dying—

Your guide to 32
European cities

scabbed in Isaiah
—Your red beard
snobbed in
  Dolmen ruins
  in the editions
  of the Bleak—

Your saints and
Consolations bereft
—Your handy volume
rolled into
        an urn—

And your father
  and mother besmeared
  at thought of you
  th'unspent begotless
    crop of worms
—You lay
  there, you
  queen for a
  day, wait
for the "fen-
  sucked fogs"
  to carp at you

Your sweety beauty
discovered by No Name
in its hidingplace

till burrs
part from you
from lack
of issue,
  sinew, all
  the rest—
Gibbering quiver
  graveyard Hoo!

The hospital
  that buries
      you
    be Baal,
    the digger
    Yorick,
& the shoveler
    groom—

My rosy tomatoes
pop squirting
  from your awful
  rotten grave—

Your profile,
    erstwhile
      Garboesque,
    mistook by earth-
    eels for some
      fjord to
        Sheol—

173

And your timid
  voice box
  strangled
  by lie-hating
    earth
            forever.

May the plighted
  Noah-clouds
      dissolve in grief
      of you—

May Red clay
    be your center,
& woven into necks,
  of hogs, boars,
  booters & pilferers
  & burned down
  with Stalin, Hitler
    & the rest—

May you bite
your lip that
  you cannot
    meet with God—
        or
Beat me to a pub
      —Amen

The Almoner,
   his cup hath
    no bottom,
    nor I
     a brim.

Devil, get thee
back
  to russet caves.

August 31, 1965, Florida